ISABEL THOMAS

CREATE YOUR OWN CHRISTMAS

ILLUSTRATED BY
KATIE ABEY

Christmas comes but once a year.
So it's FAR too important to leave
to Santa, a bunch of elves and
your family to get it right.

It's time to take control of your festive destiny.

This book is packed with activities
that use each page in a different way.

It's not one of those Zzzzzzzzzzz activity books
that's all about sitting quietly and doodling penguins.
Get ready to colour, cut and construct as you
CREATE YOUR OWN CHRISTMAS!

HOW TO ~~USE~~ WRECK THIS BOOK

Tell your parents to sit down with a good read (such as your present list), and leave it all to you. Start by making the Advent Calendar (page 3). Let the countdown to Christmas begin!

BUILD DAZZLING DECORATIONS (PAGE 7)

FOLD YOUR OWN SNOWBALL FIGHT (PAGE 49)

CREATE CROWNS AND CRACKERS (PAGES 21 AND 35)

LAUNCH SANTA INTO THE AIR (PAGE 53)

Extra kit:

Most projects just use scissors, glue and pens or pencils. These boxes tell you if you need any extra kit:

Cut the paper along these lines

Fold the paper along the lines

Look out for this icon — these pages will completely self-destruct, so make sure you read every word before getting started!

THIS PAGE GETS DESTROYED!

ELF AND SAFETY INFORMATION

All the projects in this book have been designed to be safe for children to carry out at home, if they are confident with using scissors. We recommend that an adult helps out with or supervises certain projects, including Christmas Dinner Art, Christmas Critters, Sleigh Launcher and Snowball Fight. When launching Santa's Sleigh (page 53) make sure that it is pointed away from other people and never directed towards eyes. For Christmas Dinner Art (page 13) an adult should make the paints using hot or boiling water, and children should not use the paints until they have cooled down to room temperature. Make sure that children don't taste or eat paints made with food.

CHRISTMASOLOGY

If you're serious about building the best Christmas ever, check out the Christmasology boxes. You'll discover the history and science behind the best day of the year.

ADVENT CALENDAR

THIS PAGE GETS DESTROYED!

Countdown to Christmas morning in style, by making this advent calendar. Its nifty dial means you only have to make one door...

Extra kit:
- Scissors • Pencil • Paper fastener

What to do:

1. Carefully cut along the solid line on page 5 to remove the page from the book.

2. Cut out the three windows and two slits. Use the point of a pencil to make a hole through the place marked with a cross.

3. Cut out the circle on this page. Make a hole at the centre of the circle with a pencil.

4. Hold the circle with 1st December facing upwards. Slide it behind the front of the calendar so the points marked with a cross line up. Push the paper fastener through the pencil holes to hold the pieces together.

5. Turn the paper over and fold the paper fastener down to hold the circle in place.

6. Cut out the slider shape on this page. Fold along the dotted lines.

C   D

12th   1st
11th
20   19   18
21   17   2nd
10th   22   16   3rd
9th   23   X   15   4th
24   14
13
8th   5th
7th   6th

E

7. Fold flaps C and D inwards, so they lie on top of the long strip. Starting from the front of the calendar, feed the long strip of paper marked E through slit A (a). Pass the strip behind the circle and out through slit B (b).

8. Fold flaps C and D out again to hold the mechanism in place (b).

9. Lastly, fold along the dotted line to hide the circle of paper and the slider inside the calendar.

10. Check that your calendar is working. The door should lie closed over the window and pop open when you pull tab E (c).

11. Turn the wheel to set the calendar to 1st December. Flex those festive fingers – it's ready to use!

A

B

C

Why is 6 December afraid of 7 December?

Because 7 8 9!

24th 13th

23rd 14th

22nd 15th

21st 16th

20th 17th

19th 18th

7 6 8 5 9 4 X 3 10 2 11 1 12

DANCING DECORATIONS

These spinning trees will make sure your radiators don't miss out on the fun!

THIS PAGE GETS DESTROYED!

Extra kit:

- Scissors
- Colouring pencils
- Thread
- Sticky tape

What to do:

1. Colour the spiral shapes then cut them out along the thick black lines. Cut especially carefully around the middle part: this bit is fiddly!

2. Make a small hole in the centre of each spiral, in the place marked with a cross.

3. Knot a length of thread through the hole. Ask an adult to help hang the tree over a radiator (NOT touching the radiator, but around 10 cm above it).

4. When the radiator is on, watch your decorations dance!

X

X

CHALLENGE
Try making the trees out of spare wrapping paper.

CHRISTMASOLOGY

When air is heated, its particles spread out. This makes the warmer air less dense than the cooler air around it. The warmer air rises upwards (just as an object less dense than water floats to the surface). As the warm air rises, it pushes on the Christmas tree and makes it spin. Cooler air from other parts of the room rushes in to take the place of the warm air, gets heated by the radiator and rises. This means that the spinning never stops!

Haven't you finished that scarf yet?

I keep dropping my needles.

WARNING

Don't put the trees over an electric heater or open fire or candle or any other type of heat source that is not a radiator. Always check with an adult first.

GALLOPING REINDEER

Make a reindeer decoration that gallops across your bedroom wall.

CHALLENGE

Use the cardboard shapes as templates to make a whole herd of galloping reindeer.

Extra kit:

- Scissors
- Sticky tape
- Hole punch
- Two paper fasteners
- Three lengths of string or wool, two 5cm lengths and one 15cm length
- Small bead with a hole

What to do:

1. Cut out the reindeer and his legs from inside the back cover.
2. Use a hole punch to make a hole in each set of legs, in the place marked with a circle.
3. Attach the legs by pushing a paper fastener through the front of the reindeer's body, then through the hole on the leg.
4. Arrange the legs so they are pointing straight down. Tape the short piece of string between the crosses on the legs, above the paper fasteners.
5. Tie the longer piece of string to the very centre of the short piece. Tie a bead to the bottom of the string.
6. Finally, tape a short loop of string on to the reindeer's back so you can hang him on a wall or door.

WHO NAMED SANTA'S REINDEER?

Dasher, Dancer, Prancer, Vixen, Comet, Cupid, Donder and Blitzen were named in a poem called *'Twas the Night Before Christmas*, written in 1823. Donder is sometimes called Donner. Rudolph the Red-nosed Reindeer joined the team almost 100 years later. He was dreamed up as a character for a children's colouring book in 1939, then became the star of a cartoon and one of the best-selling Christmas songs ever. Rudolph was almost called Reginald or Rollo!

Which of Santa's reindeer couldn't see a thing?

No eye deer.

POP-UP CHRISTMAS CARDS

Learn the secret behind these easy-peasy pop-up Christmas cards.

Extra kit:

- Scissors
- Coloured card or paper
- Glue

What to do:

1. Cut out a rectangle from page 11.

2. Fold the paper in half, bringing the short edges together.

3. Cut along the solid lines, then fold along the dotted lines and crease firmly (a).

4. This is the fiddly part. Open the paper up and push the folded flaps inwards, so they end up folded INSIDE the card (b). Open up the card to reveal your 3D block art. Add your Christmas message.

5. Fold a piece of coloured card or paper in half. Glue your block art inside (c).

Once you've learnt the trick, design your own block art cards. You can build anything with a few cuts and folds!

What do you call a group of penguins at the North Pole?

Lost

CHRISTMASOLOGY

The Victorians started the trend for Christmas cards: the world's first Christmas cards were sold in 1843. The people who received these first cards were luckier than they knew — one was later sold at auction for £20,000!

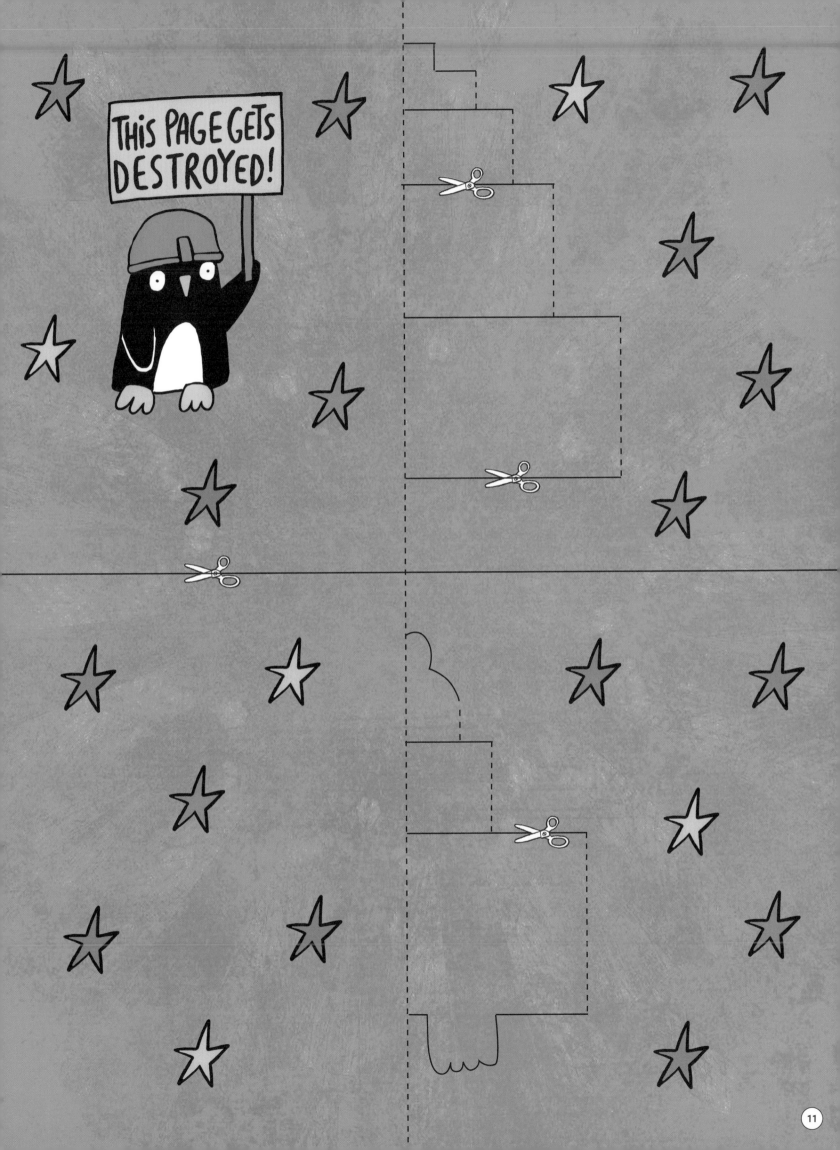

LEFTOVER CHRISTMAS DINNER ART

They tell you not to play with your food... but they didn't say anything about painting with it!

RED: cranberries

ORANGE: onion skins, grated carrot

YELLOW: sage

GREEN: brussels sprouts, greens

PURPLE: red cabbage

BROWN: coffee, tea, gravy granules

BLACK: charcoal (if the turkey timing is badly wrong — otherwise, snaffle the coal buttons from a snowman)

Extra kit:

- Adult helper
- Leftover Christmas dinner ingredients (see the list to the left)
- Small pots
- Hot water
- Sieve
- Paintbrush

WARNING
Do not eat or drink your paints, not even if they are made from food. Keep them away from young children.

What to do:

1. Pick a food from the list. Grate, tear or crumble it into a small, waterproof container.
2. Ask an adult to pour a little hot water into the container (just enough to cover the food).
3. Leave the container until it is completely cool, then strain to remove the pieces of food.
4. Use your paints to finish this festive painting!

CHRISTMAS PUDDING

Traditional Christmas puddings were packed with surprises. What will you hide in your pudding-shaped gift box?

Extra kit:
- Scissors

What to do:

1. Cut out the template on page 15, including the small slits.
2. Fold along the dotted lines (a).
3. Pinch the holly leaves together (b).
4. Fold up one of the remaining sides, and post the holly leaves through the slit (c).
5. Add your gift, wrapped in tissue paper (d).
6. Fold up the last side of the pudding, posting the holly leaves through the slit to hold the box closed (e).

A

B

C

D

E

LIST OF TINY GIFTS:

Lone jellybean

Single Lego brick

Penny coin

Priceless diamond

Add your ideas for tiny gifts

So hard to choose...

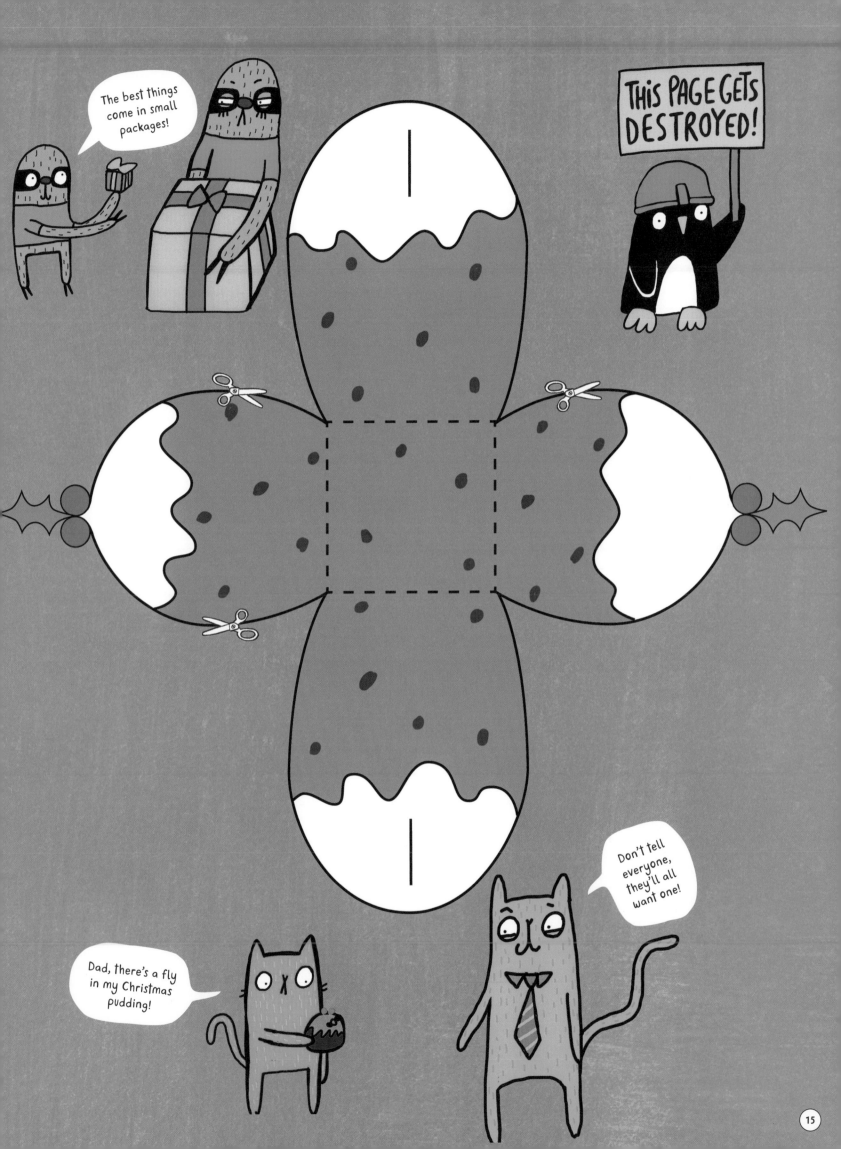

Is it supposed to be so crunchy?

CHRISTMASOLOGY

A coin is traditionally dropped into the Christmas pudding to bring one family member good luck for the next year. That's not all the Victorians snuck into their Christmas pudding mix. Some families added a wishbone to bring wealth, a ring to bring romance and an anchor to bring safety. One less lucky person would find a thimble — a symbol that they would have a super thrifty year mending everyone's socks.

Extra kit:

- Pencil
- Colouring pens or pencils
- Rubber

What to do:

1. Colour in the large triangle. Get ready to grow it into a snowflake!

2. Divide each side of the triangle into three equal lengths. Draw and colour a smaller version of the same triangle on each of the three sides, to make a new shape with 12 sides.

3. Divide each of these 12 sides into three equal lengths. Draw and colour in a smaller triangle at the centre of each 12 sides, to make a new shape with 48 sides.

4. Divide each of the 48 sides into three equal lengths. Draw and colour in a smaller triangle at the centre of each of the 48 sides, to make a new shape with 192 sides!

5. At this point you can give up and find some chocolate OR you can repeat the process again, this time adding a new triangle at the centre of each of the 192 sides!

PERFECT SNOWFLAKE

Channel your inner mathematician by making a fantastic festive fractal.

CHRISTMASOLOGY

This page shows you how to make a PERFECT snowflake. By drawing the same shape over and over again, at smaller and smaller sizes, you have made a fractal.

Real snowflakes are made up of tiny ice crystals with six sides. Like fractals, the crystals are arranged in repeating patterns to build all kinds of beautiful shapes.

EVERGREEN WREATH

Don't forget your bedroom when you deck the halls! Decorate your door with this easy-peasy Christmas wreath.

Despite being made of SPIKEY holly, POISONOUS yew and DEADLY berries, traditional evergreen wreaths are actually a symbol of joy to welcome guests to the house!

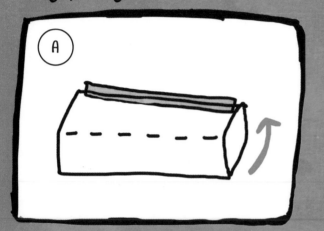

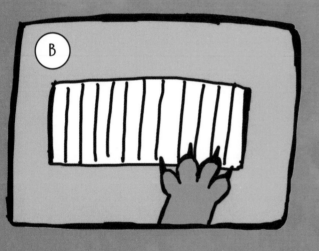

Extra kit:

- Scissors
- Sticky tape
- Sequins, glitter, pom poms, paper decorations (optional)

What to do:

1. Cut page 19 out of the book. Fold it in half lengthways and open it out.

2. Fold both long edges in to meet along the central line, so they just overlap (a). Tape them together along their length.

3. Open out the shape and fold along the crease you made in step 1 to flatten it back into a long rectangle. The side covered in solid lines should be facing upwards.

4. Starting at the fold, cut along the solid lines, stopping at the end of each line (b).

5. Carefully open up the shape to make a tunnel (c).

6. Bend the tunnel into a circle and join the ends with tape (d).

7. Decorate the wreath with paper candy canes and bows, or add glitter and pom poms.

8. Hang it on your bedroom door.

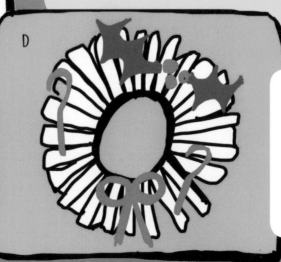

Traditional wreaths are decorated with natural things like fruit and pinecones. You can decorate your wreath with whatever you like!

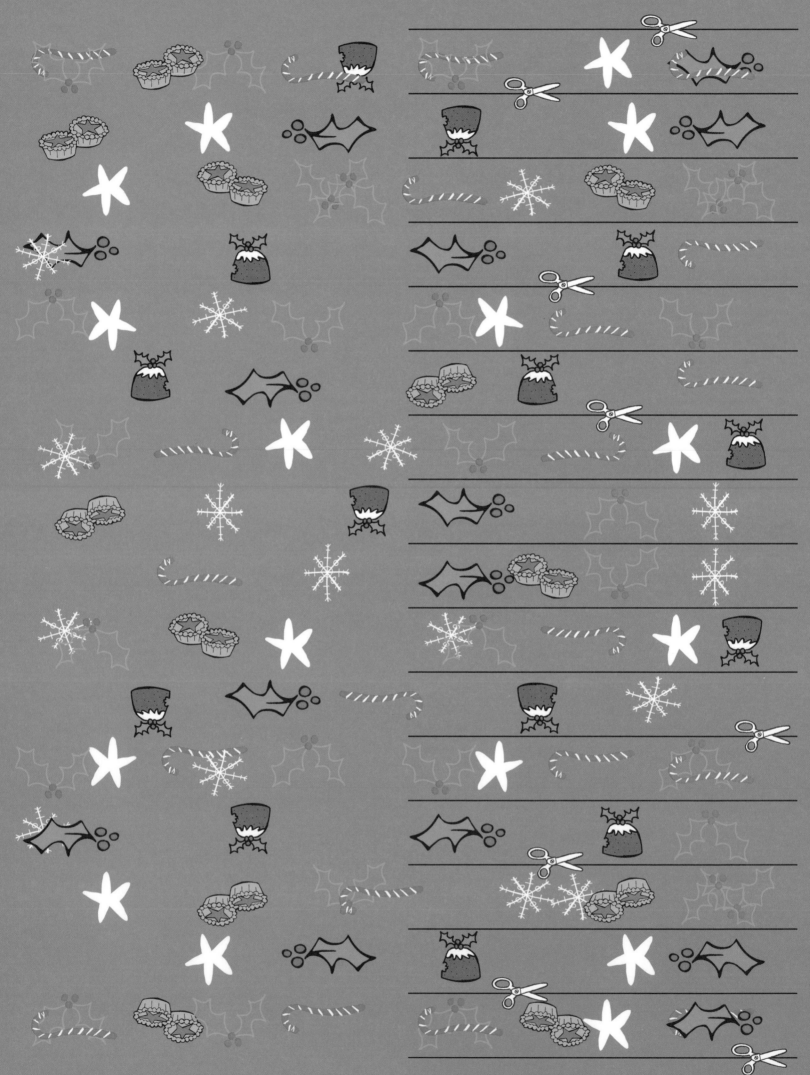

CHRISTMAS CRACKER

Christmas feasts start with a BANG thanks to crackers. It's easy to make your own.

Extra kit:

- Scissors
- Thin cardboard tube(s)
- Sticky tape
- String, wool or ribbon
- Cracker snaps (optional – you can ask an adult to order these online for a few pence)

What to do:

1. Carefully remove page 23 from the book. Lay it with the patterned side down on the table (a). Fold along both dotted lines. Carefully snip out the small triangle shapes, cutting through both layers of paper (b). Unfold the paper (c). Cut out the large triangles at each end.

2. Cut the cardboard tubes into three pieces: two pieces measuring 4 cm, and one longer piece measuring 12 cm (d).

3. Put the three cardboard tubes on the paper in the places shown. Use a little tape to keep them in place.

4. If you are using a snap, feed it through the tubes so the snap is in the middle tube. Trim the ends if you need to.

5. Roll the paper tightly around the tubes and tape it in place (e).

6. Tie a piece of string around the outside of the cracker, between two of the tubes. Knot tightly so the paper comes together.

7. Drop jokes and treats in through the open end. (Take a look at page 22 for inspiration!)

8. Tie a second piece of string between the other two tubes.

BANG!

CHALLENGE

Make more crackers using old wrapping paper. You can decorate them with sequins, buttons and ribbons.

CHRISTMASOLOGY

The bang is a tiny explosion. The explosive ingredient is silver fulminate, a substance made by reacting silver with acid. But if you're thinking about dropping your granny's best spoons in a vat of vinegar, STOP! Silver fulminate can only be made in labs and is INCREDIBLY EXPLOSIVE and INCREDIBILY DANGEROUS. A Christmas cracker contains a TINY amount: less than a tenth of a thousandth of a gram, sandwiched between two long strips of card. When you pull the strips in opposite directions, the silver fulminate moves across a rough piece of sandpaper. The heat generated by friction makes the compound explode!

> Crackers were invented by a Victorian sweet maker. He wanted to make a wrapper that snapped as you opened it, to remind people of the crackle and snap of a log fire.

BAD JOKES BANK

It wouldn't be Christmas without a bad joke. Slip these into your homemade crackers.

What's black and white and red all over? A sunburned penguin	Where do you find three-legged reindeer? Wherever you left them
What's red and white and goes up and down? Santa on a pogo stick	What falls at Christmas but doesn't get hurt? Snow
Why did Santa lose his voice? He had tinsellitis	What does Father Christmas do in the garden? Hoe Hoe Hoe

DANGLING CHRISTMAS TREE

You know paper is made from trees - but have you ever seen a tree made from paper? Scissors at the ready to make one in under a minute!

THIS PAGE GETS DESTROYED!

Extra kit:

- Scissors
- Thread
- Sticky tape
- Sequins (optional)

What to do:

1. Cut out the circular template below.

2. Fold it in half to make a semicircle, and in half again to make a quarter circle. Make sure the line markings are on top.

3. Carefully cut along the white lines, stopping when you get to the end of each line. Cut along the black lines, stopping when you get to the end of each line.

4. Gently open up the shape to make a circle again.

5. Fold the two central triangles up and pinch them between your fingers. Lift your hand up to open up the Christmas tree shape.

6. Make a small hole through the two small, central triangles, and push some thread through.

7. Secure with sticky tape and hang the tree from a ceiling or doorframe.

8. Decorate the tree with sequins.

A BAD TIME TO BE A FIR TREE

People have been decorating their homes with evergreen plants — think holly and ivy — for hundreds of years. In the mid-1800s, the British Royal Family started the trend for dragging a whole tree inside! Queen Victoria's husband, Prince Albert, decorated the palace with trees just like the ones he'd seen as a child in Germany. British families began to copy the idea — soon every home had a tree decorated with candles and sweets. From there it spread to the USA, and December officially became a Bad Time To Be A Fir Tree.

Extra kit:

- Scissors
- Sticky tape

What to do:

1. Cut out the strips of paper at the foot of this page. Give two strips to a friend, and keep two strips for yourself. Challenge your friend to make a paper chain in the fastest time.

2. While your friend links their loops together, you should make just one loop. Before you join the ends together, secretly put a complete (360°) twist in the paper (a).

3. Announce that you have won (b). When everyone complains, say that you have actually made a two-loop chain – and you will prove it.

4. Take a pair of scissors and cut down the line at the centre of the loop. Keep going until you get back to the place you started (c).

5. Watch as one loop becomes two!

6. You can do the same with the other loop, and make a chain of four loops, while your friend has only two!

THIS PAGE GETS DESTROYED!

A

B

Cut all the way along the line to cut the strip in half.

C

LAZY PAPER CHAINS

Wow your friends and family with the lazy way to make paper chains.

What happens when you cut all the way around the centre of a Mobius strip? What happens if you cut along a line a third of the way in from the edge?

CHALLENGE

Experiment with making paper loops in different ways. Try giving the paper a half twist (180°) before joining the ends. This turns the boring, flat two-sided piece of paper into an awesome one-sided object known as a Mobius strip. To prove that it has one side, draw a line down the centre of the loop without taking the pen off the paper. You will arrive back where you started!

BRILLIANT BAUBLE

Join the dots to make a dazzling decoration.

Extra kit:
- Pens or pencils
- Ruler or straight edge

What to do:

1. Look at the pairs of numbers below. Join each pair with a straight line: for example, join number 1 and number 9. Then join number 2 and number 10. And so on... Tick each box as you go.

2. This should reveal a secret decoration. Now colour in your creation!

- ☐ 1 →9
- ☐ 2 →10
- ☐ 3 →11
- ☐ 4 →12
- ☐ 5 →13
- ☐ 6 →14
- ☐ 7 →15
- ☐ 8 →16
- ☐ 9 →17
- ☐ 17 →25

- ☐ 18 →26
- ☐ 19 →27
- ☐ 20 →28
- ☐ 21 →29
- ☐ 22 →30

- ☐ 23 →31
- ☐ 24 →32
- ☐ 25 →1
- ☐ 8 →31

- ☐ 7 →29
- ☐ 6 →27
- ☐ 5 →25
- ☐ 4 →23

- ☐ 3 →21
- ☐ 2 →19
- ☐ 3 →26
- ☐ 5 →27

- ☐ 7 →28
- ☐ 9 →29
- ☐ 11 →30
- ☐ 13 →31
- ☐ 15 →32

- ☐ 17 →24
- ☐ 17 →23
- ☐ 17 →22
- ☐ 17 →21
- ☐ 17 →20
- ☐ 17 →10
- ☐ 17 →11
- ☐ 17 →12
- ☐ 17 →13
- ☐ 17 →14

MESSAGE IN A SNOWFLAKE

If you find Christmas cards a bit yawnsome, send secret snowflake messages instead!

Extra kit:

- Scissors
- Pen
- Saucer of water

What to do:

1. Cut out one of the square templates on page 31.
2. Fold along the dotted lines numbered 1 to 4 in order.
3. Cut along line 5 to chop the top off the shape (a).
4. Cut out the shaded areas (get an adult to help with this step).
5. Open up your snowflake (b).
6. Write a festive greeting at the centre (c).
7. Fold the arms of the snowflake to the centre, one by one (d).
8. Carefully float the snowflake on a saucer of water, flat side down. Watch the snowflake unfold in 'snow motion' to reveal your message (e)!

CHRISTMASOLOGY

Paper is made of fibres with microscopic gaps between them. Water is drawn up into these gaps, causing the creased paper to swell up and unfold.

Experiment by making snowflakes with different kinds of paper.

WOO XMAS!

WOO XMAS!

30

THIS PAGE GETS DESTROYED!

31

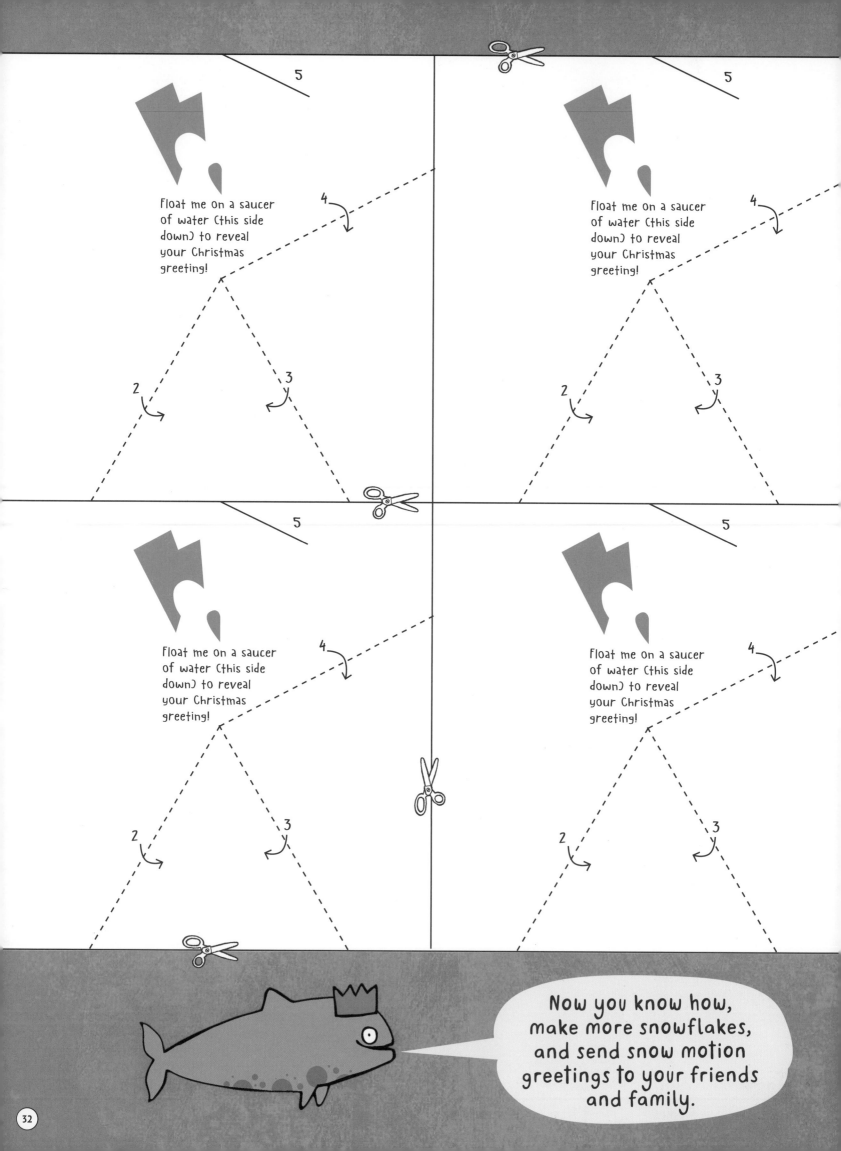

ROCKING ROBIN

You've never seen a robin rock like this before! See if anyone can guess the secret behind its rocking, rolling moves.

Extra kit:

- Scissors
- Colouring pens
- Sticky tape
- Marble

(A)

What to do:

1. Cut the robin template from this page. Colour the feathers brown.

2. With the red side up, fold the beak backwards, towards the eyes. Turn the template over.

3. Bring the ends of the long strip together, so the end with the beak completely overlaps the shaded area. Use sticky tape to hold the ends together (a). The beak should stick out.

4. Fold up one of the sides and tape it in place.

5. Put the marble inside the robin.

6. Fold up the other side and tape it in place.

7. Cut out the wings. Fold along the dashed lines. Tape the top of the wings to the sides of the robin. The bottom of the wings should stick out.

8. Put your robin on a flat surface and give him a push to start him rocking and rolling.

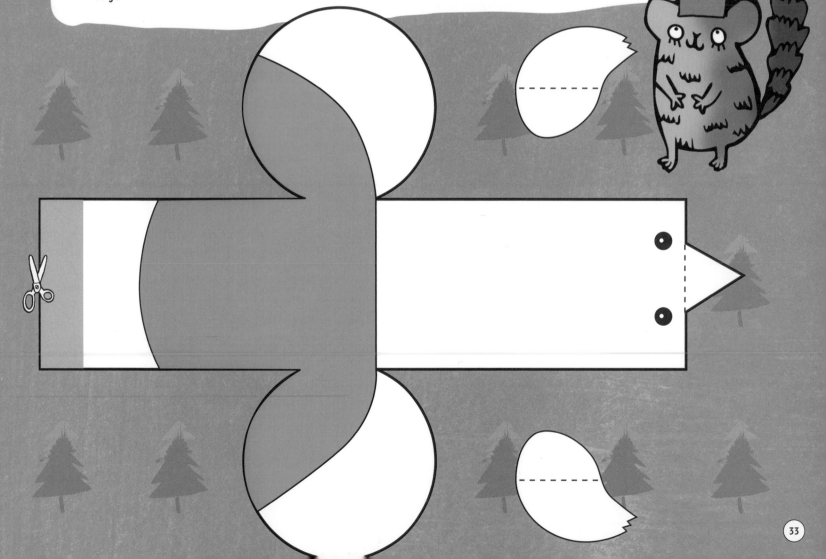

CHRISTMASOLOGY

The European robin is a star of Christmas cards around the world. It may be thanks to the bird's famous red breast — the first postmen to deliver Christmas cards wore red waistcoats and were nicknamed 'robins'. In Europe, listen out for robins singing loudly around Christmastime, as they look for mates.

PARTY CROWNS

This project will help you recycle the ENORMOUS pile of wrapping paper that fills the room on Christmas morning.

THIS PAGE GETS DESTROYED!

For instructions on how to make these party crowns, turn to page 37!

This template will make a mini party hat. Use it to decorate an orange for the Christmas table! Add cloves to make a mouth, eyes and nose, or add some of the funny decorations on page 39.

Extra kit:

- Scissors
- Square of wrapping paper or tissue paper

What to do:

1. Cut out the square of paper on page 36 and place it on a flat surface, bee side up. Fold the paper in half along fold line 1, and unfold.

2. Fold the paper in half again, along fold line 2. This time, keep it folded.

3. Fold the shortest sides (fold lines 3) in to meet at the centre (a).

4. Fold one of the corners down (fold line 4) and unfold (b). Now grab the flap marked with a dot and open up that flap, flattening along the creases you just made to make a triangle (c).

5. Repeat step 4 with the other flap.

6. Turn the paper over. Fold each of the short sides (fold lines 6) into the centre (d).

7. Fold the bottom front corner flaps up to the centre (fold lines 7). This will make a large triangle. Fold the triangle up over the top half of the shape.

8. Turn the paper over and repeat step 7 on the other side (e) (fold lines 8).

9. Put your thumbs inside the pocket and gently pull apart. Squish the centre down a little to make a crown with four points (f).

It's a great way to recycle leftover wrapping paper. Decorate your guests AND save the planet before lunch!

A

B

C

D

D

E

F

Follow these instructions, using the template on page 36. Once you've mastered it, go back to step 1 and use your spare wrapping paper to make a larger crown. Repeat to make enough for everyone on Christmas day!

To make a party crown fit for a king (or you!), start with a square of wrapping paper or tissue paper measuring 60 cm by 60 cm.

WHY DO WE WEAR SILLY HATS AT CHRISTMAS?

Travel back in time 2,000 years, and you'll find the Ancient Romans swapping gifts, putting up decorations, overeating and wearing cone-shaped hats. They were celebrating Saturnalia, a feast named after the Ancient Roman god Saturn (the planet was also named after him). Like Christmas, Saturnalia took place at the end of December to brighten up the cold, dark winter. People wore pointed hats to show that everyone was equal during the celebrations. The idea caught on, and in the 1800s, paper hats were added to the first Christmas crackers. For one day a year, we are all kings and queens!

CHRISTMAS CRITTERS

What's made of wool but is 100% more exciting than a Christmas jumper? A Christmas critter! Use this page to make woolly critters for the fluffiest Christmas EVER.

Add lots of layers for a fluffier critter.

Extra kit:

- Scissors
- Wool - lots of it!
- Glue and glitter (optional)

What to do:

1. Cut out the critter templates from the inside front cover.

2. Place one C shape directly on top of the other. Wrap wool around the templates, working your way to the end and back again until they are covered in a thick layer of wool (a). If you run out of wool, knot a new piece on and keep going.

3. Use scissors to snip a path through the wool all along the edges of the cardboard. Pull the templates apart very slightly (b).

4. Take a long piece of wool and carefully wrap it around the C shape, sliding it between the cardboard layers. Knot the wool tightly, pulling all of the threads together at the centre of the C shape (c). Remove the cardboard and fluff up your woolly critter (d).

5. For inspiration on how to decorate your critter, or to make a larger Christmas critter, turn to page 39...

To make a bigger or smaller woolly critter, use bigger or smaller templates. The bigger the template, the more wool you will need.

(A)

(B)

(C)

(D)

Here are some ideas to bring your Christmas critters to life! Use them as decorations, stocking fillers or gifts. Make your own decorations based on the drawings on this page.

Roll your critter in a very thin layer of glue then sprinkle with glitter to make a snowflake

Create a window full of white critters, hanging down like snow

Build a reindeer (two brown critters stuck together with a tiny red woollen nose)

Make a snowman (large white critter and smaller white critter with accessories)

Create a robin (large and small brown pom poms with felt belly and paper eyes and beak)

Construct the world's fluffiest nativity scene

Cook up a fluffy Christmas pudding (brown critter with green paper leaves and white paper 'icing' decoration)

Make a penguin (black critter with white felt belly, paper eyes, beak and flippers)

STUFFABLE STOCKINGS

Fold a spare pair of Christmas stockings to leave out for Santa. They make great tree decorations too.

Extra kit:

- Scissors
- Wool or string
- Small gift (perhaps a wrapped chocolate or sweet)

What to do:

1. Carefully cut a rectangular template from page 41.

2. With the patterned side up, fold a small strip of paper over at the top (fold line 2) (a). Crease firmly and turn the paper over.

3. Fold the right hand third of the paper across to the left (fold line 3).

4. Fold the left hand third of the paper across to the right (fold line 4). Tuck the very top of this flap underneath the white strip at the top of the flap you made in step 3 (b).

5. Fold along the dotted horizontal line (fold line 5), crease, and unfold. Fold along the dotted diagonal line (fold line 6) (c), crease, and unfold.

6. Slip your index finger underneath the top layer of paper. Lift the paper up and across to the right hand side, opening the layers out and squashing the paper flat along the creases you made in step 5, so you get the shape in picture 'd'.

7. Fold the paper back along the dotted line (fold line 7) (e).

8. Fold the top flap down over the bottom flap (fold line 8) (f). It's beginning to look a lot like Christmas!

9. Fold over the very corners of the toe (fold lines 9) (g), crease and unfold. Open up the toe and use the creases to push the paper in on itself to hide the corners inside the toe (h).

10. Fold the very corners of the heel inside the flaps to make a rounded corner (i).

11. Open up the top of your stocking and pop a small gift inside. You can stand your stocking up on a table, or tape a small loop of wool or string inside and hang it on the Christmas tree.

Make more paper stockings from leftover scraps of wrapping paper. Pop a small gift inside each one!

Tuck under →

2

7 ↷ →

↷ 6

5 ↷ →

Tuck under →

2

7 ↷ →

↷ 6

5 ↷ →

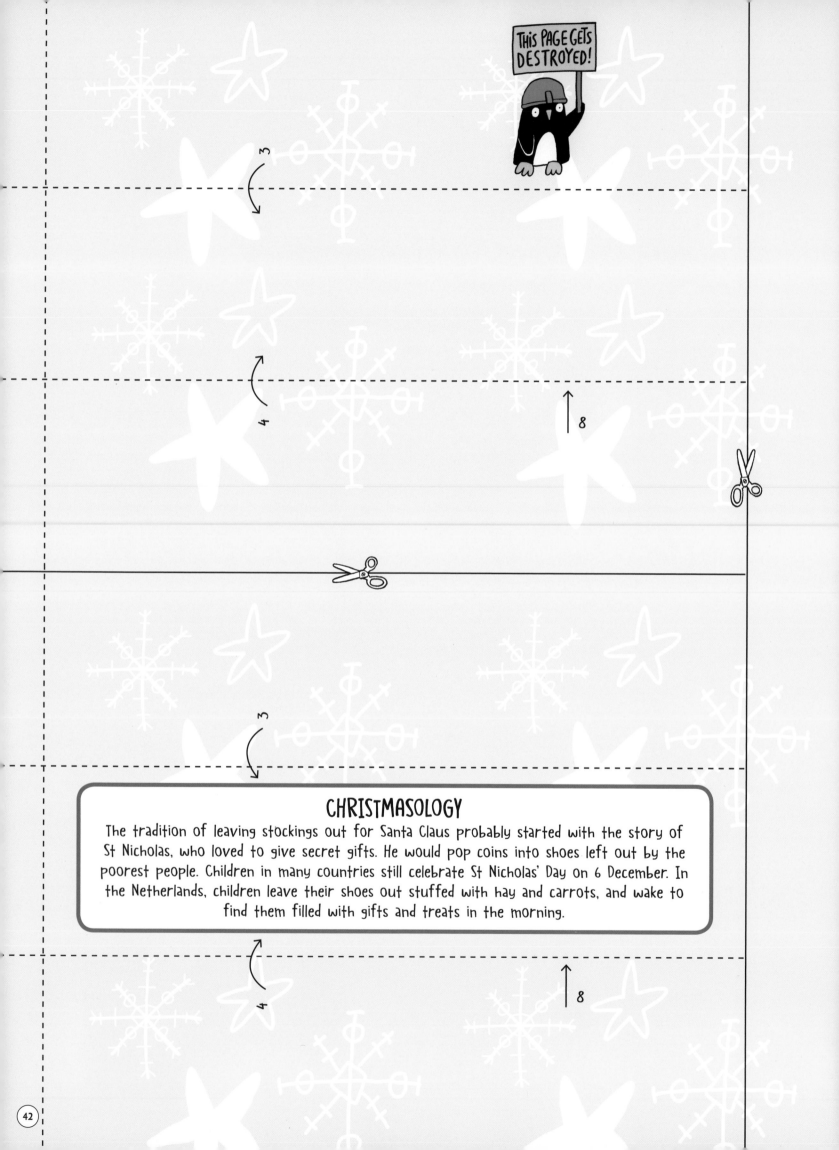

CHRISTMASOLOGY

The tradition of leaving stockings out for Santa Claus probably started with the story of St Nicholas, who loved to give secret gifts. He would pop coins into shoes left out by the poorest people. Children in many countries still celebrate St Nicholas' Day on 6 December. In the Netherlands, children leave their shoes out stuffed with hay and carrots, and wake to find them filled with gifts and treats in the morning.

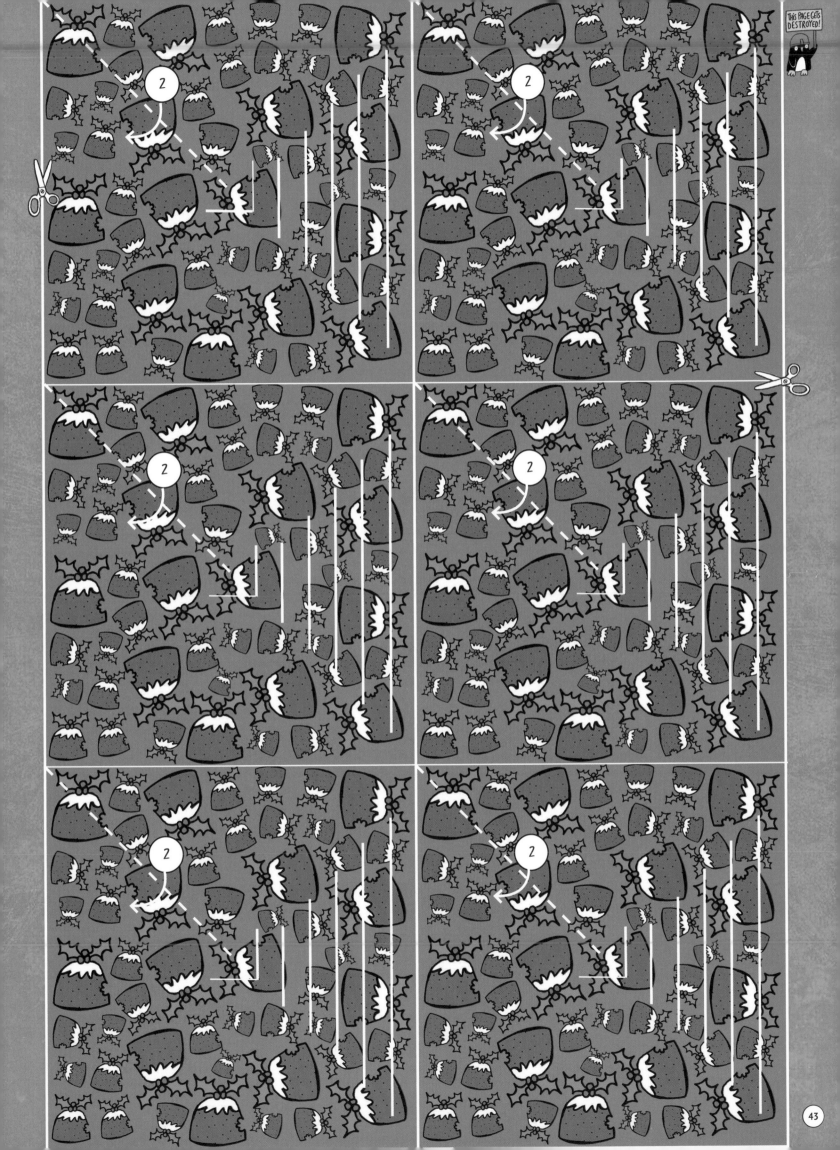

SHINING STAR

Christmas trees are often topped with a star. This one will make your tree the best-dressed in town.

SAFETY WARNING: Never hang paper ornaments near heaters, open fires, lights, fairy lights or candles. They could catch fire easily.

Extra kit:
- Scissors
- Sticky tape or glue
- Thread

What to do:

1. Cut out a square template from page 44. Fold it in half (fold line 1) to make a triangle and in half again (fold line 2) to make a smaller triangle. The lines should be on the outside.
2. Cut along the solid lines. Make sure you stop at the end of each line (a)!
3. Unfold the paper so you have a flat square again (b).
4. Working on one side, take the innermost triangles. Bring them together, curving them so that one point lies on top of the other. Tape them in place (c).
5. Repeat with every other pair of triangles (d).
6. Turn the shape over and repeat on the other side, matching up the remaining pairs (e).
7. Repeat steps 1 to 6 with the remaining templates.
8. Use thread to join the points at one end to make a six-pointed star.

A

B

C

D

E

CHRISTMASOLOGY

A star has a 'starring' role in the Christmas story, or nativity. In a time before social media, maps and sat navs, it's a star that gets everyone to the right place at the right time.

The world's best-lit Christmas tree had more than half a million lights – including a 1.5-metre-wide star made up of 12,000 light bulbs!

WOBBLING, GOBBLING TURKEY

Make a wobbling, gobbling turkey decoration for the centre of the table.

Mum, can I have a puppy for Christmas?

Certainly not. You can have turkey like everyone else!

People haven't always eaten turkey at Christmas. Popular dishes of the past included goose, swan, pheasant and even peacock! Until the 1950s, turkeys were only eaten by wealthy people. King Henry VIII was the first monarch to gobble up a turkey for Christmas dinner, making it the fashionable thing to do.

OFF WITH HIS HEAD!

Extra kit:

- Scissors
- Sticky tape and glue
- Colouring pens or pencils

What to do:

1. Cut out the turkey body templates from inside the front cover.

2. Cut along the solid lines to make a narrow slit in each piece. Slide them together.

3. Make the turkey's ruffled tail from the wide strips on page 47. Cut out the two grey strips and concertina fold each one along its length.

4. Tape one end of one concertina to the shaded area on one side of the turkey's body.

5. Unfold the concertina to make a semicircle. Tape the end of the concertina to the shaded area at the top of the turkey's body. It will stick up above the body.

6. Repeat steps 4 and 5 with the second concertina. Join the two together at the top to complete the circle.

7. Make the legs using the four narrow strips on page 47. Cut out a pair of strips. Lay one end on top of the other at right angles. Fold the strips over one another alternately until you run out of paper. You will have made a paper spring.

8. Cut out a foot and stick it to one end of the spring. Tape the other end of the spring to the turkey's body.

9. Repeat steps 7 and 8 to make the other leg.

10. Perch your turkey on the table, or on a shelf with his wobbly legs hanging down.

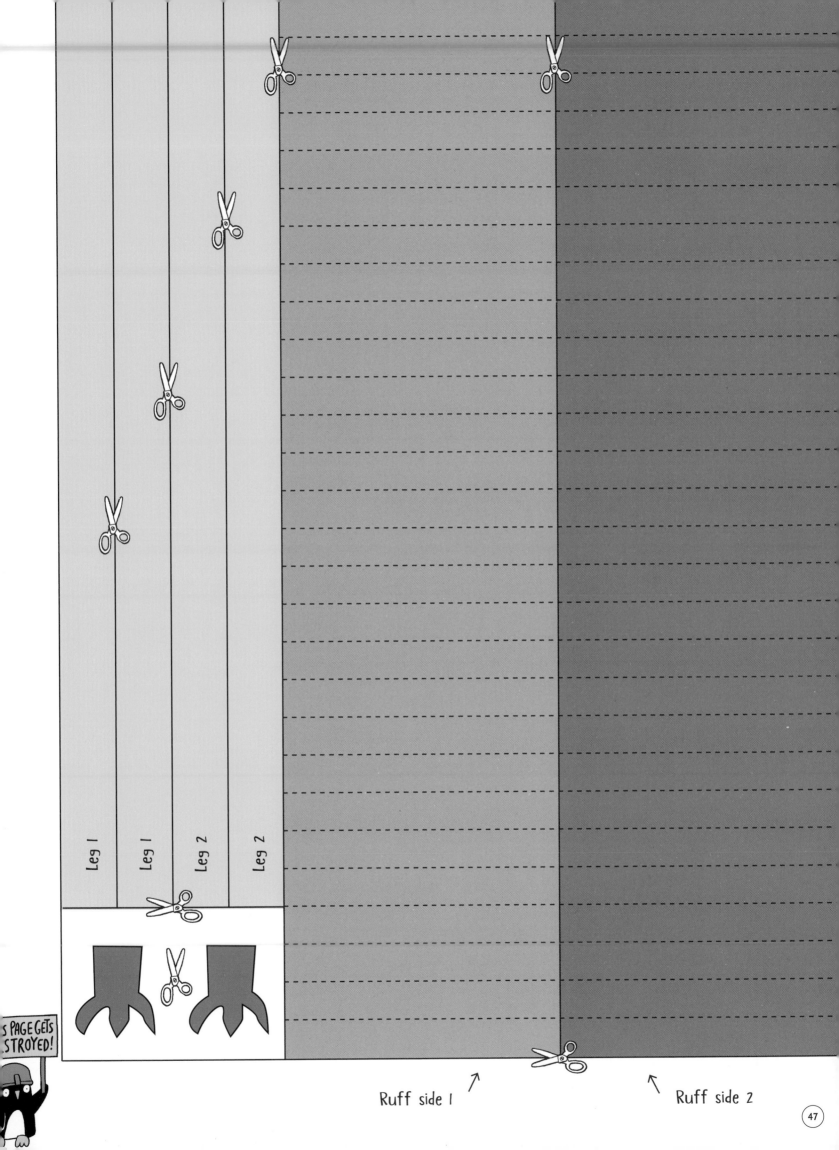

Leg 1

Leg 1

Leg 2

Leg 2

Ruff side 1

Ruff side 2

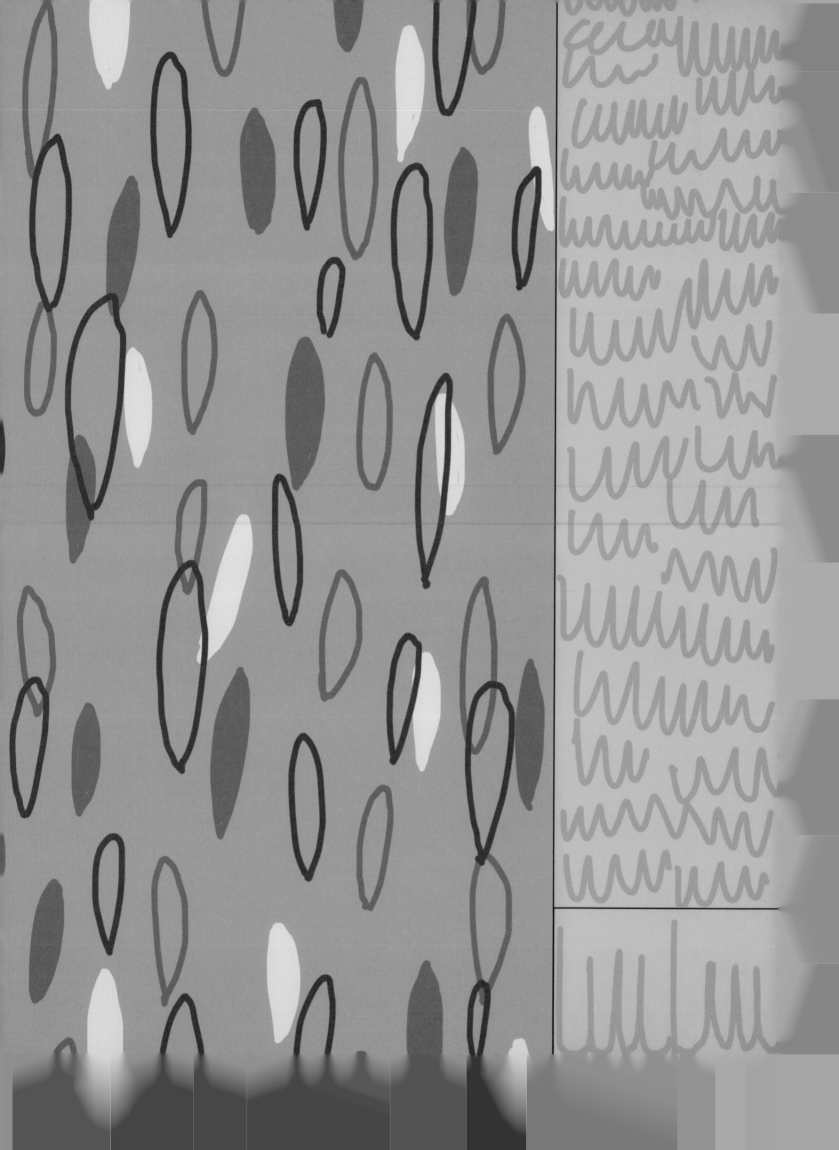

SNOWBALL FIGHT

It's not Christmas without a snowball fight... but don't wait until it snows. Build your own SUPER SOAKER paper snowballs!

Ho, ho... OH!

Extra kit:

- Scissors

What to do:

1. Cut out the square template on page 51. Fold the paper in half from top to bottom (fold line 1) and left to right (fold line 2), then unfold (a).

2. Turn the paper over. Fold along each diagonal line (fold lines 3 and 4), then unfold (a).

3. Turn the paper so the corner marked with a star points towards you. Fold the bottom corner to the top corner (fold line 2) to make a triangle (b).

4. Pinch the bottom corners of the triangle and push them together gently (c). The paper will start to make a star shape (d).

5. Bring the points of the star together in pairs and flatten, to form a triangle with the big snowflake on top.

6. Turn the paper so the point of the triangle points away from you (e).

7. Working with the top layer of paper only, fold along the dashed lines (f) so the bottom edges of the triangles meet in the middle. Turn the paper over and repeat on the other side, to make a diamond (g).

8. Working with the top layer only, fold the left and right hand points of the diamond in to meet in the middle (h).

A

B

C

D

E

F

G

H

More instructions this way!

9. This will make two little pockets. Tuck the top points into these pockets. Turn the paper over and repeat steps 8 and 9 on the other side (i).

10. Pick up the paper and find the little hole at one of the pointed ends (j). Blow into it gently to inflate your snowball (k)!

11. To turn it into a super soaker snowball, trickle water in carefully through the hole. Go outside and splat your snowball on the ground!

I

J

K

CHALLENGE

String paper snowballs together to make a festive garland.

Build a big batch of snowballs and arrange a Christmas day snowball fight!

RULES OF ENGAGEMENT

* Don't throw snowballs at anyone's face

* Don't throw snowballs at anyone who hasn't given you a Christmas present yet (they might change their mind)

* Don't throw snowballs at unsuspecting passers-by (especially those wearing red and white suits and carrying sacks full of gifts)

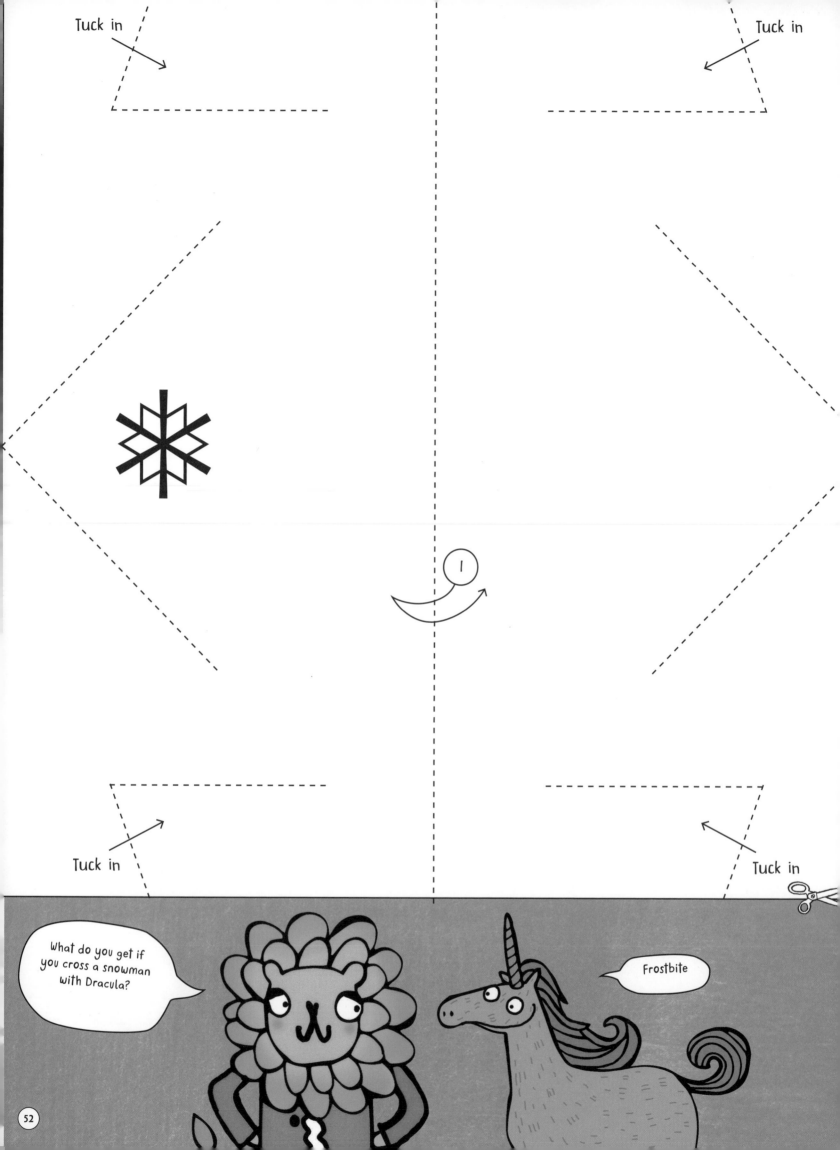

SLEIGH LAUNCHER

Help Santa get around the world in record time by making this catapult-powered sleigh!

THIS PAGE GETS DESTROYED!

Extra kit:

- Scissors
- Sticky tape
- Small elastic band

What to do:

1. Carefully cut page 55 out of the book.

2. Fold along fold line 1 and unfold.

3. Fold the two top corners down to lie along the crease (fold lines 2 and 3). You will make a triangle at the top of the paper (a).

4. Fold the triangle down over the rest of the paper (fold line 4).

5. Fold the top corners down (fold lines 5) so they meet at the centre (b).

6. Fold the point of the triangle up so it covers the corners (fold line 6).

7. Now fold the sleigh in half along the original centre crease (fold 7), hiding the folds you made in steps 4 to 6 (c).

A

B

C

D

More instructions this way

8. Fold each 'wing' down along fold line 8 and up along fold line 9 (d).

9. Use a piece of sticky tape to hold the sides together, so your sleigh looks like picture (e).

10. Cut out the Santa template on this page. Fold along the dotted line and tape him in place on the sleigh.

11. Cut out the small notch marked at the base of the plane (f).

12. On Christmas Eve, launch Santa by looping one end of the elastic band over the notch, and the other over your finger. Pull the sleigh gently backwards and release to send it flying... reindeer free!

E

F

ELF AND SAFETY:

Don't overstretch the elastic band, or it could snap and hurt somebody. Aim the plane and the band away from people and pets. Always be very careful using elastic bands near eyes. Young children should wear eye protection.

What goes oh, oh, oh?

Santa's sleigh reversing!

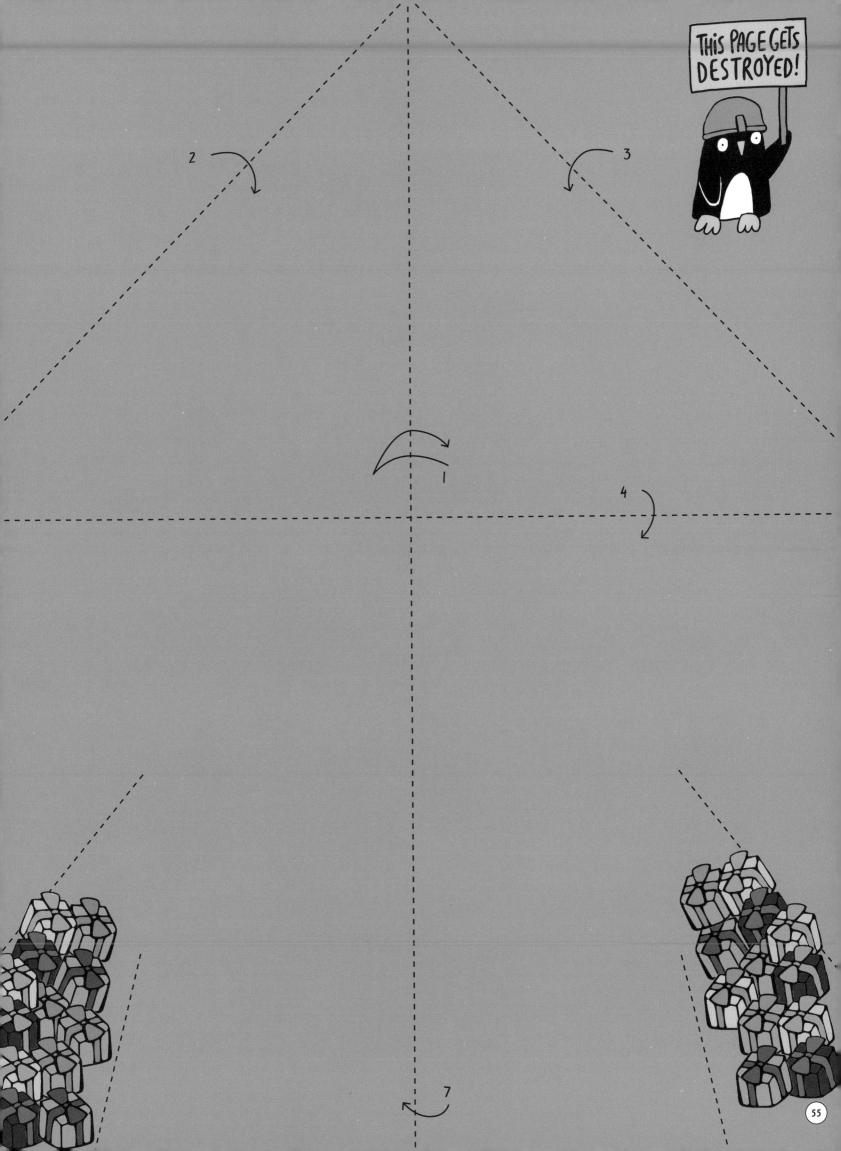

THIS PAGE GETS DESTROYED!

55

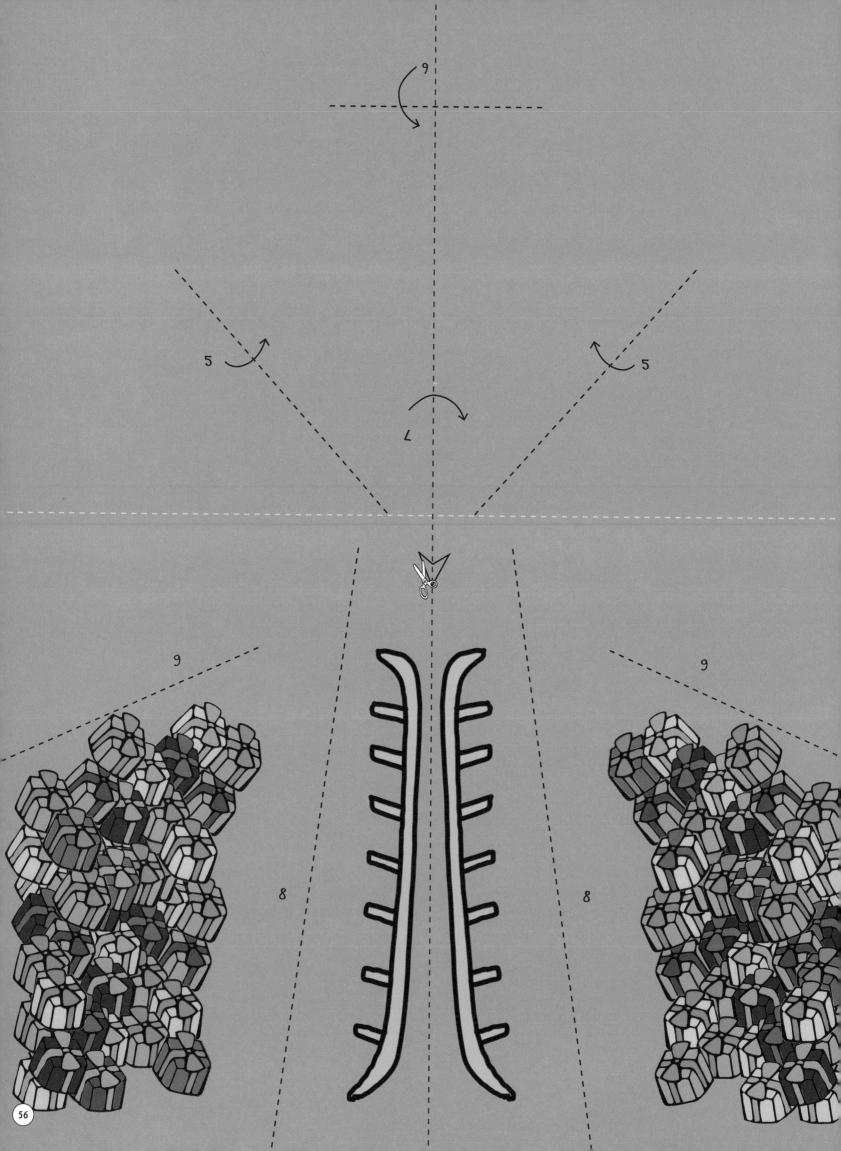

SCROOGE GIFT TAGS

THIS PAGE GETS DESTROYED!

What's the best thing to give your parents at Christmas?

A list of the presents you want!

These funny gift tags might shock your family and friends – before putting a smile on their faces! Turn over to find out more.

Have a terrific & unbeatable Christmas full of satsumas!

Wishing you and your family an awesome and joyful Christmas in your pyjamas!

You look **AMAZING** like a Christmas sprite ready to go out **DANCING!**

Terrific, incredible present inside, sent in time to get on your good side!

We Hope and wish that you get nothing but the thing you **MOST** want!

Red-nosed reindeer dropped this amazing gift off for YOU!

You're going to be jumping to the MOON when you discover how much you like this present!

I'm so HAPPY to CELEBRATE Christmas by giving amazing gifts to you!

Extra kit:
- Scissors
- Sticky tape

What to do:
1. Cut out a gift tag.
2. Fold each one in half and crease firmly.
3. Fold the top flap back on itself to meet the right hand edge. Crease firmly.
4. Attach the tags to your gifts.
5. Pull the cracker to reveal the real message and go from Scrooge to Santa!

Wishing you an aw ful Christmas!

Wishing you and your awesome and Christmas in your family joy an ful pyjamas!

GUESS WHO GAME

Everyone loves a silly game at Christmas. Use these masks to give your games a fancy dress twist!

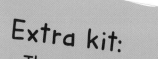

THIS PAGE GETS DESTROYED!

Extra kit:

- Thin cardboard
- Glue
- Scissors

What to do:

1. Stick this page (this side down) on a piece of thin cardboard. (Make sure you read all the instructions first!) When the glue is dry, cut out the masks, including the slot for the nose.

2. To play the game, give everyone a mask. They must hold it face down, and put it on without looking at it.

3. Ask everyone to put on their mask at the same time by pushing their nose gently into the slot.

4. Everyone must ask questions to try and work out who they are. Each question should have a yes/no answer, e.g. Am I an animal? Am I cold?

5. A person can use their turn to try and guess who they are. If they get it wrong they miss their next turn.

6. Work around the table, asking one question at a time, until everyone has guessed which character they are.

Am I Santa Claws?

PRESENT DROP

THIS PAGE GETS DESTROYED!

Extra kit:
- Scissors
- Dice

What to do:

1. Carefully remove this page from the book. Cut out the parcels for each player. (Read everything on this page first!)

2. Put all the parcels at the North Pole.

3. Take it in turns to roll the dice, and follow the numbered paths to move one of your presents out of the North Pole and across the board.

4. When you reach a chimney, that present is delivered and can be removed from the board.

5. A player can have more than one of their presents out for delivery at once.

6. If you land on another person's present, they are moved back to the North Pole.

7. The winner is the first person to deliver all of their presents!

We got hold of Santa's top secret route network and used it to make this game. It will keep your family busy while you hunt for hidden presents.

Doctor doctor, I was making my Christmas list and I swallowed the pen!

Use a pencil instead

SCRAMBLING SANTA

Help Santa climb chimneys a bit faster, with the help of friction.

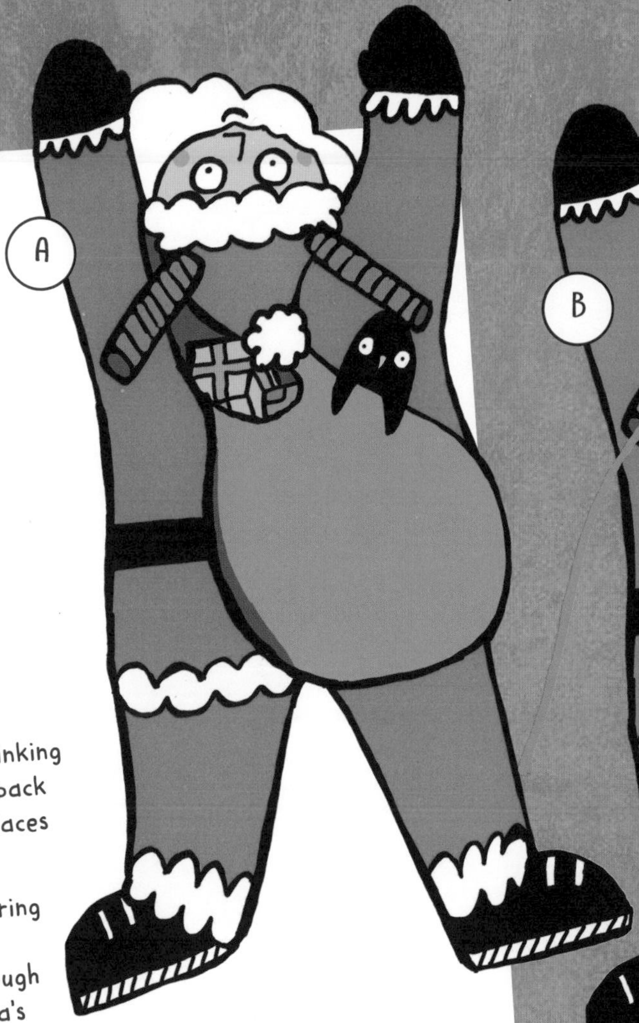

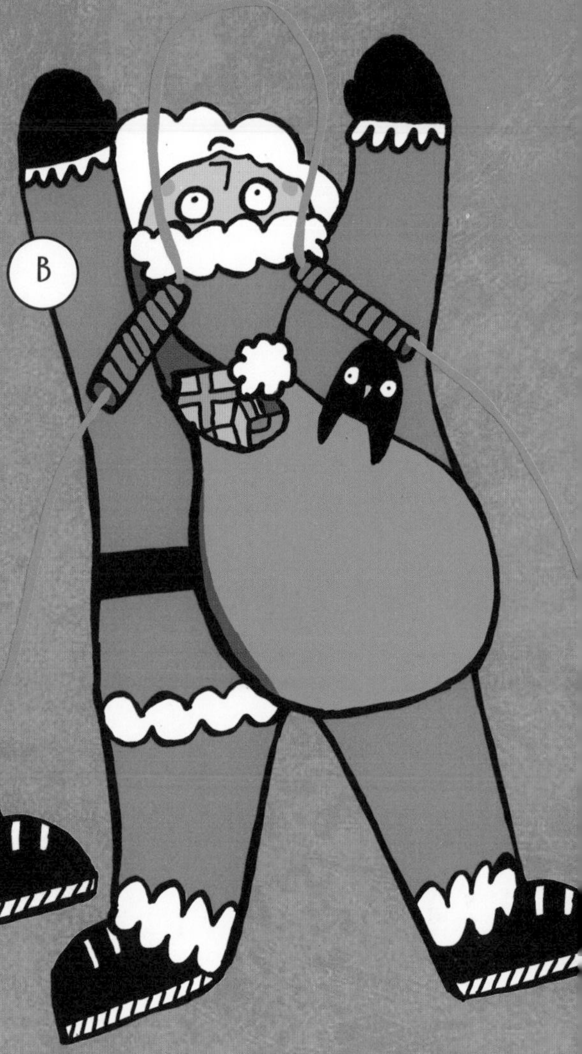

Extra kit:

- Scissors
- Drinking straw
- Sticky tape
- Wool or string
- Two beads

What to do:

1. Cut the Scrambling Santa template from the inside back cover.

2. Cut two 5 cm pieces of drinking straw. Stick them to the back of the template, in the places shown here (a).

3. Cut a piece of wool or string around 2 metres long. Thread the wool up through one straw towards Santa's head, then down through the other towards his feet (b).

4. Tie a bead or washer to each end of the wool or string.

5. Loop the thread over a hook or nail. Move Santa to the bottom of the string and grasp one end of the string in each hand.

6. Pull one hand straight down, letting the other hand move upwards. Alternate hands like this to make Santa climb the chimney!

(A)

(B)

What would you give a six-foot, 400 lb gorilla for Christmas?

Anything he wants!

CHRISTMASOLOGY

Santa climbs the string thanks to friction — a force that tries to stop one surface sliding across another. Each time you pull a string straight down, Santa moves to the opposite side so the string lines up with the straw. That string moves easily through the straw. On the other side, the string presses against the straw. This increases the friction between the string and the straw, and Santa travels up with the string instead of sliding down. When you swap hands, the same happens the opposite side. Santa gradually climbs the chimney.

CHALLENGE

Experiment with the load in Santa's sack by sticking on a coin. What is the maximum load he can carry up the chimney?

CHALLENGE

Experiment using different types of wool, thread or string to find out if changing the material affects the frictional force.